Contents

What are wings?

Wings are part of a body.

Some animals have wings.

Wings are joined to the sides of an animal's body.

Why do animals have wings?

Most animals that have wings can fly.

Some animals with wings cannot fly.
These penguins cannot fly.

Different wings

Wings come in many shapes and sizes.

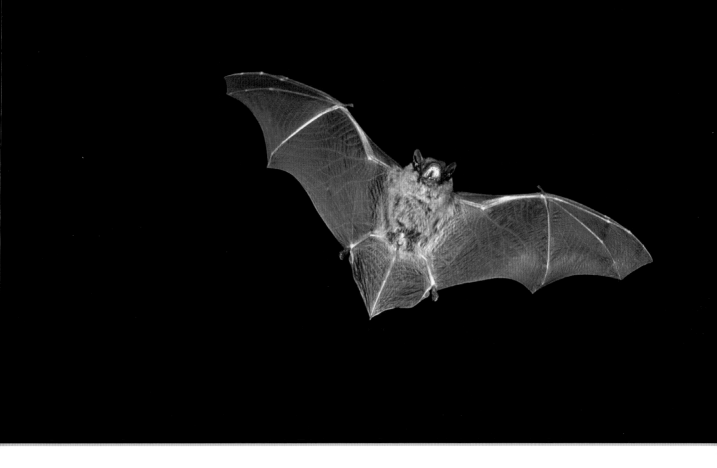

This is a bat.

It has thin skin on its wings.

wingspan

This is an albatross.

It has a very big wingspan.

This is a bee.

It has a very small wingspan.

Can you spot the difference?

This is a ladybird.
It has small wings.

This is a dragonfly.
It has four wings.

Amazing wings

This is a vulture.
It can fly very high.

This is a falcon.
It can fly very fast.

This is a hummingbird.
Its wings move very fast.

This is a penguin.

Its wings help it swim.

Can you spot the difference?

This is a butterfly.

Its wings have pretty colours.

This is a cormorant.

It dries its wings in the sun.

Do people have wings?

People do not have wings.

They use their legs and feet to move.

People can use their arms to move through water.

Can you remember?

Which animal uses its wings to move through water?

Picture glossary

 **cormorant** a large, black sea bird

 **dragonfly** a long, thin insect with double wings

 **wingspan** size from the tip of one wing to the tip of the other

Index

Notes for parents and teachers

Before reading

Talk to the children about animals with wings. Have they seen birds flap their wings and fly? Talk about animals that have wings but which are not birds (such as bats, insects). What makes a bird special is that its wings are made of feathers. Talk about animals that have wings but do not fly (such as penguins, ostriches, emus, or kiwis).

After reading

• Buy a bag of coloured feathers from an art shop. Hold a feather in your hand and stick your hand up as high as you can in the air. Let the feather float down to the floor. Talk to the children about how the feather is light and the air supports it. Explain how birds use the feathers on their wings to support them. Drop a ball from the same height and compare how it falls to the floor.

• Draw an outline of a bird and ask the children to stick feathers it. Talk about putting the smaller feathers on the body and the longer feathers on the wings. Explain how to place the feathers in the same direction.

• Say the rhyme with the hand actions: Two little dicky birds sitting on a wall (hands clenched, both thumbs bending up and down). One named Peter (just bend right thumb), one named Paul (just bend left thumb). Fly away, Peter (make right hand do flapping motion like a wing and hide it behind your back). Fly away, Paul (repeat with left hand). Come back, Peter (reverse the flying action with right hand). Come back, Paul (reverse the action with the left hand).